Hurricane Girl

Hurricane Girl

ANNA SCHENCK

REALLY SERIOUS LIT 2023

Published by Really Serious Literature

ISBN: 978-1-0881-1191-8

THE PART WHERE I COMPARE MYSELF
TO A GAS STATION TOILET

I find myself admiring gas station bathrooms. Often so, in the same exact way one would show affection for a piece of art. I draw some sort of reflection from it. The cracked tiles, and walls littered with words etched from a marker guided by Parkinson's. Weird stains on the ceiling. And I, in some way, want to photograph this place. Yes, the toilet looks like it belongs in a prison but it stands there fixed in the center of this havoc, unapologetically it's own.

Perhaps it is the necessity of it all.

For who really desires to use a gas station bathroom unless they are in dire need of it?

You're in the middle of nowhere on this journey and you're so desperate to relieve yourself, that you'd do it most anywhere.

And then...the gas station toilet presents itself.

And that's the same way I see most of you men. You're impatient and everything you do is so ill-timed, that the minute you're able to let go and find relief, you'll do so anywhere. And usually, you'll come to me, in the dark of the night—around 2 am—trying to tell me about your mother, and the girl you last loved, and why you hate Coldplay. And I'm just another girl to slide your fingers and your secrets into until the booze leaves you colder and more alone than before. But right now, at 2:02 am, I am your best comfort and your biggest need.

I am chaotic, and marked up, and scarred and I'm grateful that you won't notice any of these details at the moment. I already know what your weight feels like on me and how your breathing shortens when you talk about your second year in college because that was the year you lost your best friend. I already know if I was to ask you to love me, you would say, "Anna, you're just too complex to love." And I already know that's code for..."You're hot, but you're crazy" or "you're funny but you're too sad."

The funniest people are the saddest, you idiot.

I will stand fast, in the middle of your havoc, like a porcelain beacon, helping you extrude your sadness until it becomes that all too familiar emptiness you are so accustomed to.

You will feel better, no doubt. You will flush away all the memories of our time together...embarrassed by the interaction. The desperation of it all.

I will whirl and gurgle about, reminding you that I may be tossed aside, but never forgotten.

And you will continue about your day....until you eat the wrong tray of sushi... or the wrong woman...

And I'll be here, waiting.

JOE

Joe is a schmuck.

Joe is an old Seabee who likes
hanging around the same pub as I

He will always
buy me my third cider of the evening,
no matter who he is with

"thank you for your service!"
He shouts his gratitude
and all I can do is politely accept it

Joe got mad at me last week
because I talked about anal
and cheating husbands

"You wouldn't cheat
if you had a wife like that, Joe?"
I was referring to the loud woman
who did nothing but talk about workplace gossip
She kept making fun of her husband.

I made our bartender go over
and see if his phone was overturned.
"Joe, if his phone is turned
upside down, he's cheating,"
Joe rolls his eyes.
And buys me a third cider.

Oh, Joe.
Old and sad and cynical.
And yet, fatherly and curious.

He asks me if I'm okay.
I tell him "I can handle
alcohol like I'm John Wayne."

He laughs,
and laughs.

Joe.

Maybe I'm the schmuck.

RECYCLE BIN HEARTBEAT

I am peanut butter spoon-fed religion wishing my words would stop sticking to the roof of my mouth.

You are smooth-talking, syrup-sucking sailor man slithering your way into the last particles of my existence, expecting a blissful journey. And a journey you shall receive

We will embark at 11pm because I don't want to see your face in natural daylight. Daylight is for good things. Like picnics, and blowing bubbles with barefooted children or mowing your lawn with a cool Coors.

And you are not a good thing, sailor man or maybe you are. But my sweet baby face houses a brain that's hell-bent on making you a villain. But the most handsome villain you shall be.

At 1142, we will be slightly buzzed from the moonshine and the moonlight and you will tell me things... sacred things.

Like how you always wanted a girl to stick her thumb up your ass.
Or about how you're terrified of jellyfish.
And of course, I promise not to tell anyone.
And I haven't...

At 1153, I'll tell you how my mom and I used to make shadows of our feet against the ceiling on evenings when my dad was gone. And to you, this is just a sweet memory but to me, it is the foundation of my being. The epitome of my happiness. And you're just another heartbeat of a recycle bin in which I dump my fondest memories, hoping you can hold them for me.

At 1237, we will be drunk and obliterated and I will now pretend you are anyone else other than who you claim to be. You hold my hips as we dance. And you are just an object. An object to hold me up as I sway to the same clubby remix of the same Chainsmokers song in the same heels and the same dress that I've been stuffed into for the last year.

At 0112, You'll whisper something sexy in my ear but all I hear is the deep whining that perpetually graces every man's lips on a drunken weekend. And I hate you so much more than anything on this earth right now, but I whisper back about "wanting you inside of me" or some bullshit that I read in Cosmo when I was 12.

At 0156, we stumble into your apartment that smells like axe and burritos and you'll undoubtedly have an x-box which you'll talk about and I'll wish I had paid more attention in Home-Ec so I'd know how to sew your lips closed. I'll come over and kiss you and slightly moan and you'll reciprocate with a full raging hard-on which I wonder how you even acquired in such a short amount of time.

At 0212, I'll be fully naked on your couch, distracted by a weird gray spot on your carpet. You'll be in the bedroom shuffling around for a condom. You'll come back and it's time for you to penetrate me and I am such a lucky gal, aren't I?

At 0214, you'll give an exasperated last gasp as you jizz inside a latex tube. You'll do that strange half-waddle to pull it off and dump it into the toilet or in the trash bin... or in a mason jar to preserve it.

At 0235, I am walking around your apartment as you snore and gurgle. I search through your medicine cabinets and your bank statements, trying to only now retrieve a sense of who you really are. Now that I know you will no longer want anything to do with me, I'm going to want everything to do with you. I see a framed photo of you and your girlfriend. She looks like her name would be Stacy or Brianna. She is tiny and her clavicle bones are prominent, creating little bowls between them and her shoulders. I have this urge to pour wine into them and lap it out with my tongue while you watch. Oh yes, I'm going to want EVERYTHING to do with you now, sailor man.

At 0324, I'll leave you quietly, no note. You'll wake up much later, and feel undeservingly satisfied and very parched. And you'll continue with your life, thinking you'll never hear from me again. And I'll continue with my life, waiting like an ill-timed menstrual period to pop back into your life. To make myself known again. But until then....until all that comes to pass...

I'll simply swipe right.

HOLE PUNCHED SKY

When I was a little girl
I would hide underneath the tables
Of my Sunday school room
And pick the lint off my little girl tights
Plastered onto my little girl legs
And I would wait for everyone to leave
So I could jump out at my teacher
And make her tell me more about Jesus

And she would sigh and oblige
And my little girl heart would be full
And my little girl brain would be flooded

And I would take my little girl self outside
And conquer my little girl world

And I would spend my days in a swing
That hung from a tree in our front yard
And I would sing softly and puncture the sky
With my little girl feet

Now Sundays are spent in a haze
Leftover from the nights I can't remember
And my little girl feet spend more time running
Rather than demolishing the clouds
And Jesus is just another man who couldn't save me

And if Jesus was known for loving the drunks
and the whores, and the demonic possessed
Then he should love me the most
And he should take his big godly arms
And wrap them around my little girl body
And not touch me in any other way
Other than in his goodness

PRINCE VALIUM

To the Man Lying Fatigued on Top of Me:

I don't know you. I probably won't ask you your last name; or even how to spell your first. All I do know is that you surely believe you scored yourself a big win tonight. You think the tequila shots, the smooth-talking and the "hard work" you demonstrated tonight paid off. You think these items earned your passage between my legs.

"That was so good," you mutter onto my shoulder.

"Mhmmm," I sigh in agreement.

I wonder how long you'll lay on top of me. I'm already sick of you. There will be characteristics you won't notice about me. You won't notice my tattoos, my many scars, or that I have three aligned freckles on my right breast. You won't notice I trace the outline of your back repeatedly. I've made it a habit to memorize the curves and lines of a man's back, rather than the features of his face. I've learned I always see more of the prior. You won't notice that as I hear you groan and feel you thrust, I have tears in my eyes. I close them and imagine you're the boy I last loved. You whisper my name. I hate that you know my name. Of course, what you don't know is that you didn't choose me. I chose you. No, not you personally, Mr. Man. But someone like you. I need you.

My room was already prepared for the aftermath of this encounter. I've written out positive sayings and notations about love and self-worth for me to wake up to. My walls are covered in art that tells a lengthy story. I have an old piece of paper quoting the stages of grief carefully tacked up above my abandoned piano. You're not a man. You're not even human to me at this point. What you are is a ritual, a process; a fix.

You see as you are focused on filling my anatomical void, I'm hell-bent on fulfilling an emotional one. But right now, I just desperately need you to roll off of me. Please. Get off of me.

You're sleeping next to me now. You didn't make small talk. You ignored me. I'm so grateful for that. I don't want to hear your voice. You start to snore softly. You're in a post-ejaculated, rum-induced coma. I like you this way. I flip over to my stomach to look at you. I wonder how many times your mother would come in to check on you during your childhood. Did she feel peaceful and satisfied as she watched you slumber? I wonder what your favorite color is. I wonder why you chose to wear a polo shirt to the bar. What holiday is your favorite? Are you in love with someone? What scares you most?

I reach out and touch your ear lobe. You don't respond at all. I wonder if this is what it will feel like with someone one day. I imagine we have children in the next room. They're sleeping soundly, happily. You recently bought me a black dress but then quickly exchanged it. You had known I'd like the red one better. You know my favorite song and every lyric to it. You know how my tears will drain from my left eye before my right once I start to cry. You know how obsessed I am with Tom Hanks.

Yet, there's a part of me that hates you. A part of me that feels like a victim. But, in all honesty, your intentions are far more true than mine. You want ass. I want your soul. I'll drop you off later and never contact you. You'll see me in town and say hello. I'll ignore you. And you'll spend some time wondering why.

So to the man lying next to me, fatigued...

I don't know you. I probably won't ask you your last name; or even how to spell your first. All I do know is that while I'm just another notch in your belt, you're just another paragraph in my story.

IT'S ALWAYS MEN LIKE YOU CAPT CLIFFE

I sit slanted, obtuse, waiting for my doctor to make his appearance. It's always the most excruciating part of the appointment. I am always so impatient. I don't know what for. There really isn't anything better I could be doing at this moment--this early. I just hate when someone demands my time of me.

I wait for what seems like 8 minutes but I calculate it to actually be three. He finally emerges.

"I apologize for the wait," he mutters under his breath, "I'm Captain Cliffe."

He is blonde and extremely handsome. He is much taller than me and is well-built. Married. His presence is warm and welcoming, almost familiar. He felt like a song I heard once as a child. I know the melody but cannot place the words.

We go through what the motions of the procedure will entail. I focus between his eyes and mouth as he lists off what's to be expected of me. He talks with his hands too much. Too theatrical for someone who went to medical school. Maybe I make him nervous. Not because I'm beautiful, but because I cannot stop staring.

"Do you have any questions for me?"

I do. Of course, I do.

I want to know if he's ever cheated on his wife. It seems like a fair question to ask of someone. Is this visit not confidential anyway? He could divulge his information as easily as I produce mine. The question weighs heavily on my tongue. I feel it filling up my closed mouth, wanting to burst through my lips. I must know if he has cheated.

I want to know if he's watched some other woman undress while his phone vibrates violently in his pocket. I want to know if he's taken another woman to his favorite restaurant, while his wife cooks alone. I want to know if he's sunk his tongue into another woman's mouth, while his wife is convinced he's working late.

Shared deceit is a powerful adhesive, isn't it? It binds you permanently in some way. Your mutual lies allow you to take root in each other, so when the tearing away comes... you're left with a bit less of yourself. And it's always men like you, isn't that so Captain Cliffe? Men who are so proud of their work. So brave. You don your medals on your uniform and your office is covered with illustrated trophies of your sweet wife and children...

There you are at Yosemite, where you proposed. She's wearing khaki capris and a cardigan, sunglasses atop her strawberry blonde hair. And you thought to yourself in the nervous seconds before the proposal "she looks lovely. I'm so happy she supported me through school. She is going to make me the happiest man."

But even the happiest of men still need to bite and tear and take, to remind them that they are still, indeed, men.

It's always men like you, Captain Cliffe,

There you are when your adoring wife gives birth to your firstborn. She is exhausted, her gown soaked, but she is glowing with pride. And you thought to yourself as you bent down to kiss her "she is so beautiful. She has made me the happiest father in this world."

But even the happiest of fathers need to bite and tear and take, to remind them that they are still, indeed, men.

It's always men like you Captain Cliffe,

There you are on your seventh anniversary. You're slow dancing in the living room, the new carpet she wanted installed squishes softly beneath your feet. She smells of vanilla and lavender since she had just bathed the children. You brush back her hair and kiss her neck. She sighs into your shoulder and you think, "She is everything. She has made me the happiest husband in the universe."

But even the happiest of husbands need to bite and tear and take, to remind them that they are still, indeed, men.

It's always men like you Captain Cliffe,

And of course, these memories will turn into moments disheveled in your brain. You'll remember her seeming distracted by nature during the proposal. Or how she brushed you away after giving birth, still in far too much pain to want affection. You'll remember your anniversary as her smelling of chicken nuggets and sweat, with no time for you. All these memories will be distorted, giving you leeway to condone your future actions. You'll put on a brave face and play martyr. You'll convince yourself as you chug your fourth beer on a Thursday, that you are a good husband. A good father. A good soldier. A good lover. A good man.

It's always men like you, Captain Cliffe,

And you'll eventually find yourself waiting impatiently for another woman's phone calls. You'll imagine yourself tearing the clothes off of her, making her your own. You'll make her feel safe and she'll make you feel wanted. Isn't that really all you wanted, Captain Cliffe? To be wanted? To be worshipped? She strokes your ego as well as your cock and you start to feel alive again. You'll find any way to see her, just to talk. Talk talk talk. You'll convince yourself you're a good friend to her as you bite her lower lip and make her moan. You're doing all of this for her. This is what she wants. You're still a good husband. A good father. A good soldier. A good lover. A good man.

It's always men like you Captain Cliffe,

And on the day your little empire comes crashing down, you'll distribute the blame evenly, neatly, like clean laundry amongst all those that loved you. You'll watch your wife shed tears, and your children will be confused, and your job in jeopardy. Your value is now questioned. Rumors buzz around you like a symphony and your heart panics in response. And your little playmate is just that again--little. Smaller and shriveled up somehow. But you have bigger things to worry about. Bigger concerns. Bigger problems. Bigger issues. No time for small things. Small women. Small women who had once made you feel so big. But of course, you're still a good husband. A good father. A good soldier. A good lover. A good man.

It's always men like you Captain Cliffe,

Isn't it?

I hear him force a cough in order to retrieve my attention.

It worked.

"Ms. Schenck, again...do you have any questions for me?"

"No, Captain Cliffe... none."

PAGE JONI MITCHELL

I asked what clouds were his favorite. I felt like it was an interesting question.

"Who has favorite clouds?"

I ignore his rhetoric.

He ignores me.

"Mine are Stratus. "I mutter… "I feel like everyone loves cumulus since they're most adaptable to shape. But not Stratus. They show up in the sky, tired, maybe hung over, not thrilled to be present, yet they put on a show. Much like one would on a Monday morning.

I'm aware I sound pretentious to us both, but I've run out of topics to discuss.

He doesn't seem interested in anything I'm saying, and perhaps that's why I keep talking. Not necessarily to fill the silence, but more to leave statements for him to remember me by when I leave him.

And I will leave him.

Soon.

The ring on my left hand has looked foreign and misplaced since the minute it was slipped on. As though I'm still a small child playing with my mother's jewelry.

I'm leaving him because I'm blaming him for this deep sense of sadness in my gut. As if it just emerged since our union. We both know it's been there for years now. He thinks that maybe the sadness is just a mask for my boredom. And maybe he's right. Maybe I've been mistaking the feelings this whole time.

He's vapid. Quite honestly I just feel that I am more interesting than him. He provides no stimuli, and therefore he demands that I shrink. "Be softer, quieter, please."

I cannot.

Any ill-fated attempt, brought on more shame and disheartenment.

He is ashamed of me. I know it. I can't say that I really fault him.

The sadness isn't stemmed from shame though...it's stemmed from boredom. We know that. We were taught that. We believe that.

Instilled from toddlerhood and religiously enforced with each passing year, we were taught to be nothing but a blank, spotless canvas. Any mark or sin is to be dissected and evaluated, much like a warped biology lesson. How could we expect this marriage to be fruitful when in all actuality we're barely allowed to speak our own thoughts? What a luxury it would be to form our own words and exchange them in any sort of understanding space.

My brain drifts off to the movie Quills. Monsieur de Sade wrote nothing but absolute smut and was imprisoned for it. The crowd of depraved men and sex-starved women begged for his freedom; aching for more literary stimulation. He continued to write and had portions of his novels smuggled out and brought to the public.

The clergy found this out and took away his writing utensils. So he improvised. Using sheets and wine as paper and ink, he still was able to smuggle out his stories. When they stripped him of bedsheets, he desperately took a knife and cut open his own flesh-using his blood as ink and his clothing as parchment. Again, he was found out. They confiscated his knives and his clothing... leaving him naked and vulnerable in every way now. Yet that could not stop the storyteller. He took to using his own excrement and the walls to get his words to be heard. They declared him mad. And yes, he was crazy. But as sick as he was, his persistence was beautiful.

The story comes to my brain quite often. And while sitting there, I wondered what lengths I would go to in order to be heard and understood so deeply. I too had made sure to strip off my clothes when demanded. I had even cut open my own flesh as well. Yet the words still carried no weight, no value. What was next? A pretty blue-eyed girl, covered in her own shit, screaming to be heard? That would never do.

I ask my husband again. "There's not a type of cloud you like better than the other?"

He pacifies me with an answer.

"Anna....

Cumulus, I guess."

THE ONE ABOUT THE OLD MAN IN TRAFFIC

I've decided to name you Fredrick

It's not your real name of course
But I'm sure you would have
already named me, "sweetie" or, "hun"

I quickly open your passenger door and crawl in
"There are too many Stanley's out here" I whisper
"I'll play Blanche and rely heavily on
a stranger's kindness."

your kindness

I'm invasive and adamantly beg you
to travel to your old home in Ohio.
Because I'm desperate for a bit of nostalgia...

nostalgia I have not ever tasted or touched
You oblige since we both have
nothing better to do on this Saturday

I'll hang my pink-toed feet out the window
and ask you when you first saw a naked woman
And what your wife's hair smelled like on any given Monday
I'll ask you why you think fear is a weakness
And explain to you that I'm simultaneously scared of nothing
And yet tremble at everything

Your ears, slowly deafening will be no match
for my loud voice that
I had continuously been instructed to muffle
Which is why I can't stop searching
your brain for more gift-wrapped memories

Tell me how your father took a belt to you
after you were caught taking his whiskey
And how you sobbed in the corner after
Remembering your uncle's words
"Boys don't cry"

So you stuffed your sadness
into glass bottles
placed carefully on your shelf

Tell me where you were
when Kennedy was shot
and I'll tell you the exact moment
I started hating sunshine.

Tell me how you beat
smoking after 50 years
and I'll tell you how
I've never been able to beat
making homes out of people

Tell me of the worst act
you've committed against someone
Show me all your ugliness
and I'll be sure to polish it up and make it pretty
I've had to repair my own porcelain backbone
in order to see this day,
so let me sink my hands
into your flesh and adjust
yours to straighten you up,
Freddie,
You carry your loneliness
in your right side pocket,
mixed in with your change and handkerchief.
So empty your pockets
and hand the contents over to me

We'll both agree that all of our heroes are dead
and I'll tell you how I played
"Over the Rainbow" every night
On an old plastic music box

You'll tell me how you dreamed of being a pilot
And I'll tell you how I begged God to give me wings

But if running away hasn't helped
I can't imagine how flying would be any better.
Huh, Freddie?

I want to walk inside your old home
and tear off the wallpaper to expose
all the secrets these walls devoured up
"Home Sweet War Zone."

I'll soak up your stories
the way you'd sop up
the grease on your plate after
inhaling your mother's Sunday roast

Let me lay out all your photographs
and bathe in your old dusty world
Let me see you when you were
less cynical, more agile
your face was handsome
and if I had met you in that time,
I would have tried to kiss you
and eventually promised you
ironed shirts and healthy babies
and silly fights when I didn't sleep enough.

I want to know about your wife and how she died
and how you could never forgive
yourself for being gone that night
Tell me how your children forget your birthday
And how you still need more than you care to ask for

We'll travel back and I know your throat
is growing closed and heavy
With all the things you want to say
But you can't say them
because you're a strong man
and "Boys Don't Cry"

So scream Freddie…
scream until your vibrato appears
as a fog on the windshield.
I know all that grief is just your love
with nowhere to go.

So scream.
It's a sunny day and nature is calm
so she cannot do the screaming for us.

You have to scream, Freddie.
I'm grateful to hold your soul
and search its rigid topography.

You'll tell me that life has been nothing but brutal.
you are now a misfit in a society
moving too fast for your dying legs.
But we're lucky, Freddie.
To be too crooked to fit in just anywhere.

I'll confess that I took your picture earlier
Because who really cares about a small old man?
the lonely are forgotten just as easily as last month's news
But I won't forget you, Freddie.

We are both trash and treasure
And what mystery is there in not knowing
which we will be to whom

But Freddie.
You should go now.
You should go now and
live the rest of your life in a hurry.
Go.
For the light has turned green.

BLUE EYED FERAL GIRL

Blue eyed baby
Girl
Blue floral dress
With the torn stockings

Black and blue
I am a young girl and cleaning my house
I am pretending it is Jerry Orbach's home
I dust every crevice more thoroughly when its

Jerry's home
I am always pretending
the home is what it isn't
Which is to say

Peaceful
I had learned young
That is when I wanted
teenage neighborhood boys'
Attention

That I could just slip off my shirt
As long as I stayed behind the fence
I had full control
They'd inquire as to my mother's whereabouts

How sweet and concerning they were

Wondering about my mother
I would lean back and smile
Then push forward against the peeling,
concealing wood

To maintain my modesty

I wanted to tell them about the cat
That roamed around
That I would occasionally steal
And slip into my bedroom

Because he needed protection

You see that's the problem

Stray
Feral
Animals
They will strut

and then run
then give in
To any protection

Blue eyed
feral
Girl

You have missed a spot

Dusting

LIPSTICK MUG THOUGHTS

One day I'm gonna come home from the clinic and kiss my husband and joke about how he's getting a beer belly. I'm going to check on the pot roast and murmur a curse word under my breath after burning my mouth testing it. And then I'm going to walk up my stairs and avoid the middle of the third step because that's the one that creaks and it irks me that I haven't yet repaired it. I'll go into my daughter's room and she'll look over her shoulder and smile. I'll sit beside her and watch her do her puzzle or play her game or read her book. I'll comb her hair with my aging fingers and ask her about her day. She'll tell me about her best friend and why she hates math this year. I'll hear her stories, and to her, they're just rantings from a second grader, but to me, they are spoken monuments of her being. Testaments of her character as

I'm saving up these moments and storing them away. And I'll learn more about her with each story and recollection and complaint. We'll eat dinner later and she'll spill her milk and my husband will not scream at her or make her feel worthless for her clumsy hands. Clumsy hands that were paired with her loud confident voice, re-enacting her second-grade stories.

She will go to sleep unbruised and untouched and my off-key voice will sing her a song. A song that I will one day find a music box to inhabit and send her off to college with.

I will tell her that her mama is fond of the rainy days but that she is truly the only sunshine I've ever loved. I will turn out her light and whisper sweetness. And everything will have been reconciled and redeemed.

LOVE ALWAYS, ZELDA

He appeared almost spectacularly in the doorframe,
He looked disheveled
Like he woke up 10 minutes ago
He always looks this way
For someone who has no clue where he's going, he's in a hurry to get there

When he needs me most I never know what to say
So I offer him a naked picture of me
Because a naked woman can solve any problem
Instead, he asks about what I'm writing
He knows the language of intimacy I need
And I always want to strangle him for speaking it

We sometimes stroll around together and watch families
Tucked inside their pretty homes with their pretty white fences
We judge them
We gawk as they sit comfortably at the table
Slurping their pot roast and infidelity
"What poor bastards" I mutter

They don't have our freedom
The power to ebb and flow out of people's lives
To lick salt off a stranger's neck before tasting the burn of tequila
To leave town at 2 am for no reason
We tell ourselves we feel sorry for them

He told me once he found me amongst the wildflowers
He imagines me there, delicate somehow
Not shouting and setting things on fire
But sitting there, in a field
Getting drunk off the warm, fragrant air

He's never told me to put my "Joan of Arc" act away
He's never wanted me pretty

He's never demanded a softer, gentler version of me
He takes my loud, consuming anger and makes a whisper of it
He lets me over-romanticize John Lennon
And tree trunks
And Dali

I pout when he doesn't write my biography for me
"I'm on a date," he hastily explains
This is still not an excuse to me
So I instruct him to slide his fingers up her
And then write out my bio
"Write about me with her cum on your fingers"

We say our final goodbye in the oddest of ways
We preserve it
the way you do when you read the last paragraph of your favorite story
For we are each other's favorite stories

"I've burnt my stockings with my cigarette again"
He follows my gaze to my legs
"Yes, you have. You're always clumsy like that"
"Too much gin."
"Never too much gin."

We wring our hands and whisper words about love and future plans
For two smooth-talking wordsmiths, we become very dumb
Mixing up our adverbs and adjectives
With meaning and sincerity
We fumble through it

And then he is off again
To a distant place that never existed
Disheveled
He has no clue where he's going
But he is in such a hurry to get there.

TEN MINUTES OF SPRING ANGST

I'm sitting just outside of the fence. I'm wearing my mother's yellow cardigan and a short gypsy skirt I bought from a thrift store. When I purchased it? I can't recall.
I just picked up a cheap bottle of wine at the corner store and am now smoking my last cigarette. I save a pack for emergencies, you know.

Emergencies ranging from the slightest bit of traffic to another personal catastrophe.

The Indian man at the corner store always scolds me for my attire. "You dress like it's the summer. It is winter still, Miss Anna. It is winter."

I chirp back with, "Maybe if I dress for the summer, the summer will come!"

He smiles at my child-like optimism and I don't have the heart to tell him I prefer the winter. The crisp, cold days, the promise of another snowfall, the darkness, and in spite of all the light, I feel myself becoming, I still want the darkness.

But today is different I suppose. Today my clothes feel extra heavy on me. It's a day where I want to crawl out of my own skin. To search for zippers on my wrists and pull up, up, and away until I can step out of my flesh like it's a too-tight party dress and I'm in a 2 am state of exhaustion.

I'm still in the dirt, besides a tipped-over garbage can. There is a group of three men across the street and to the left, working in the yard. I look over and see them all staring at me. Deliberate, perched; I feel like I'm displayed. I stare back, stoned face until they look away. I want one of them to come over and talk to me. I want to argue.

I want a fight.

I see a woman stroll passed me. Before I can greet her, she asks me how I'm doing. She seems sweet. Clothed in too many layers. With glasses and wiry brown hair.

"I wonder if I'll be like her when I'm older."

I can't wait until I'm older. I want my body to just finally match my soul. I welcome the crow's feet and gray hairs that I see now.

"heart of a child. soul of an old human. light as a feather. stiff as a board."

A man comes by not two minutes later. I almost offer him some wine, straight from the bottle.

It's not hygienic though, offering strangers your drinks.

It reminded me of being at a football game back in the fall. I saw a group of fat, balding men shooting whiskey. Without even giving it a second thought, I pulled the Jack Daniels from one man's hands and chugged more than they had.

I felt the burn trickle down my throat, hearing in fainted tones about how they thought I was a "badass" and "so sexy."

Their attention was a quick fix, I suppose. I had latched on to their buddy who was much younger by far. He and I ran away into an abandoned building. We laughed and kissed in the corners of the structure, feeling so wonderfully secluded.

Secluded.

I am still huddled away in the dirt. My cigarette is gone and I promise myself "no more."

I play with the buttons of my mother's old cardigan and wonder about her.

Saint Sandy.

I recall one time, at 22, I was cooking with her in the kitchen. I was talking about all my future plans and she seemed too distracted. This happens a bit. Not by any fault of her own...but when I'm excited about a new endeavor, I want her to be my cheerleader. So I interrupted her focus with details of my latest threesome. She pauses, shocked...but she is staring at me and seeing brown hair.

"I wonder if I'll be like her when I'm older."

I can't wait until I'm older. I want my body to just finally match my soul. I welcome the crow's feet and gray hairs that I see now.

"heart of a child. soul of an old human. light as a feather. stiff as a board."

A man comes by not two minutes later. I almost offer him some wine, straight from the bottle.

It's not hygienic though, offering strangers your drinks.

It reminded me of being at a football game back in the fall. I saw a group of fat, balding men shooting whiskey. Without even giving it a second thought, I pulled the Jack Daniels from one man's hands and chugged more than they had.

I felt the burn trickle down my throat, hearing in fainted tones about how they thought I was a "badass" and "so sexy."

Their attention was a quick fix, I suppose. I had latched on to their buddy who was much younger by far. He and I ran away into an abandoned building. We laughed and kissed in the corners of the structure, feeling so wonderfully secluded.

Secluded.

I am still huddled away in the dirt. My cigarette is gone and I promise myself "no more."

I play with the buttons of my mother's old cardigan and wonder about her.

Saint Sandy.

I recall one time, at 22, I was cooking with her in the kitchen. I was talking about all my future plans and she seemed too distracted. This happens a bit. Not by any fault of her own...but when I'm excited about a new endeavor, I want her to be my cheerleader. So I interrupted her focus with details of my latest threesome. She pauses, shocked...but she is staring at me and seeing me. All of me...and that's what I needed.

Her attention was a quick fix I guess.

I find myself playing with the dirt.

The men across the street have lost interest.

So there will be no arguments tonight.

BUTTON LAMPS FOR CHRISTMAS

I had stubbed my toe against the brick wall

My grandma Mac

Her house
had so many bricks

I would always look for cracks in them
to perhaps dislodge one, in search of a key

I had seen "The Secret Garden" too many times

Grandma Mac was a little girl
through the great depression
so her pantry was always stocked
with canned goods

spinach
and corn
and beans

I don't remember watching
her eat any of these items
I can't recall her eating at all
A year after this memory
she would go in for a minor surgery
And never wake up again.

She sent "precious moments"
button lamps for Christmas
We received the news she died,
and two days later our packages from her arrived.
I used to turn the light on
and pretend that was when she could hear me...

As though a simple change of AA batteries
could bring her back to listen to my stories

Decades later, another one
of my loved ones would send me a gift
for my birthday
He had planned to end his life
but changed his mind
so when I had received the gift

it was packed full of sentiments and memories
and premature goodbyes
I hopped on a plane
to save him

I can save anyone, you know

except...

this year
my childhood friend

well
no one could save her
I hadn't heard from her for a year
and now
she's sleeping
soundly

I remember once her mother told us
after checking in on us as little girls
that
we had fallen asleep together
with legs wrapped around each other
and arms embracing

so the next night,
B put her hands on my face
and wrapped me up
and slept soundly
safely

and now
more than anything
I want to beg her to make a different choice
and I want to be the one to put my hands on her face
and wrap her up
and we'll both sleep soundly
and safely
with the promise of an awakening
in the morning

BAPTISM

I look at her Pinterest board at times. It keeps her alive.

To me,
at least.

I do it late at night when I am exhausted and feeling nostalgic.

I can never let any of my dead friends go. I see them in grocery stores and traffic stops and crossing the road as if they emerged out of nowhere.

She was never light. She was a heavy, authoritative figure. Even in our kindergarten days, I had this respect for her that was bred straight out of fear. She was tough. And as our lives move forward, and I understood more about people-specifically about grown men- I envied her tough exterior. I wanted to trade my tear-stained floral pillow for her tough heart. I found that I could not.

There is a photo of her and I with our fingers intertwined, singing on our church stage. It's like any other photo you'd find in the mid-90s. Two pretty, Peter-Pan-collared girls smiling brightly. Not presenting a care in the world...

We had lost touch for some time, reconnecting only a few years before her death. She went radio silent one week and I just figured she needed space, as we all do from time to time.

Then I received the news on a humid spring day, weeks before finding out I was carrying my daughter. I went outside and let the hot Virginia pavement burn my feet. I screamed. I drowned myself in whiskey that night. I hated her for leaving. I missed her, yet I envied her courage to escape what I could not. I wanted to join her.

And now she's a memory growing ever so distant with each passing year.

So I look at her boards. I see the recipes and the tattoo ideas. The E.E. Cummings quotes. I do this when I miss her. When I want to remind her of something we did as children.

When I want to ask her why.

I want to print out her quotes and go see all her bucket list places. I want to keep her alive. I want us to keep our plans and make more memories. I want her to know my daughter.

I have adopted her stubborn attitude and have refused to fully let go of her.

And when I do see her again, I'll make sure to intertwine my fingers in hers... and this time we will stand there, free. We won't have anything to run away from.

MAMA

Early morning bleach
Mixed with the smell of my mother's second pot of coffee
Brewing

Early morning bleach
Smells so much different
Then the bleach plastered on tiles
In the afternoon or evening

She has her hair up in the same pink scrunchy
I've seen her in since I was three
I tell her I like her hair up better
To show off her face
She has such a thin, pretty face

I've inherited
Not only my father's temper
And childlike impatience
But also his face

But
Her face
Is structured perfectly
Just like her hands
Slender with the nails bitten down

I love her bitten nails

Almost all her perfections
She possesses a habit
A proclivity even
That she cannot quit

I have habits too

Definite proclivities
That I can not
Will not

Quit

Perhaps they are just
as innocent as her nail biting

No?
She scrubs the tub
With the same vigor
You'd demonstrate while
crossing a busy highway

I sit near her
There is so much I do not understand about this woman
I come from her but I couldn't feel more
Disconnected
More removed from her consciousness

I'm sure she feels the same
"How did I raise her to be this way?"

But mama

I don't know how you can smile like that
Or how you can doctor each heartache
With a proverb
And call it whole

I don't understand how you are not
Hungry
For something different

I can't comprehend how you can laugh
Between bites of dried-out chicken
And button-up suits
And hymns sung in decibels
I don't care for

With nods
And hand shakes
And plastered grins
With eyes that have died long before
I was even born

Mama, I don't understand your world
And I know it breaks your heart
That I've run away from it

But I ran
The same way I'd run from a
Burning building
Or an attack
Or the way you'd run across the busy highway

Scrub the tub, mama
Scrub the tub and the tile
And call it good

Faster

Make all the stains go away

How I wish you could remove the top
Of my skull
And bleach
My brain too

How different it that bleach would smell

GRAMMY

You are so much more
than "second helpings"
and "Danny Boy, the pipes,
the pipes are calling…"

And they called me back
To you
To home…

Because my running shoes are now worn

And maybe I could just sleep quietly
In the back room
With the white comforter

Maybe I could sip some tea
And tell you about the walls surrounding my heart
You'll smile
Because you have them too

But our walls are built of sand
So we pretend to enjoy tidal waves
Yet I see you outside at night
In your toolshed
Building me a dam

Please tell me of your makeup
How you are skinny dipping,
midnight chasing,
howling-at-the-moon sprite

Tell me how "good night" felt more like a threat
Then a sweet bidding

How love felt like a hot hand on fragile skin

And how affection only darkened your doorway
In a 2 am drunken stupor

You will sandwich bag seal me in your embrace
And I will be reminded
That the day I was born,
You took splinters of your soul
And embedded them into mine

You have made me
Sweet yet volatile
Messy and true

And we'll thank Danny Boy
In his glen to glen
For calling me back to you.

KITCHEN

Watch me earn love
With soft hands burning
soft foods for your soft belly,

I am perfect this way.
Plastered smile with teeth bare
like the keys of a piano
I've long ago abandoned.

I am a little girl inside
a big girl body that I no longer
am allowed to cut open.

But I've found that if I look at you
with my big eyes and stupid plastered smile,
I am charming enough
to earn 22.8 minutes of affection.

When quiet feels deafening
and chaos is home
and I can hear my dead Jesus whisper

"you did good, kid"

Because you did good...kid.

Kid, you did good. Kid.

Kid.

And I'll take another swig
because sober feels like the wrong side
of naked and drunk feels
like the left side of the attic

he could never find me in.

Kid.

And I think I need just one more
glass because there's that memory
stuck about rough hands on soft skin
and I think this Rose'
should have been labeled eraser.

Kid.

And I keep cutting up
these carrots but maybe
cut the frontal part of my brain
out and fry it up
into a delicacy and serve it.

But I'm sure it'll need more salt.

Kid!

We're taught to cry "fire"
instead of rape
that's why I've made things
burn since I was a kid.

Kid.

The oven is at 350 degrees
I kept help but wonder
what our Sylvia was thinking
before she put her head in the heat.

Because, of course,
she wasn't trying to kill herself.
Maybe she was just wanting
to melt away her memory.

Kid.

But I am clichéd Cinderella story
mixed with too many pills.
And fairy godmother is a flask.
And prince charming is 3 steps away
from prancing out that heavy door. And...

Kid!

Bake the damn pie.

I SWAM TODAY

I swam today
I undressed and put on a proper suit
and went to a proper pool and dove in

I'm a mother now

So this wasn't a huge body of water
I was not naked
or drunk

I wasn't trespassing
I swam
with pool pass in hand and body recently rinsed
I swam

The year my dad left my mother flew us to the east coast
I would barge into my grandmother's pool and bury myself
underneath chlorine drenched waves
To the bottom
I'd lay on my back
and open my eyes

They would burn
my beautiful blue eyes
that I'd inherited from my runaway father
would become reddened
but I'd lay there
and watch the light dance in the waters
I couldn't hear
but more importantly
Feel
and there was my safe haven
My peaceful drowning

Now I cannot shut out the dancing light
though I wish to,
while the water looms in my ears and enhances all my thoughts
They spill out echo in to stinging chlorine waves

Yet I swim

The lifeguards watch me
They are German.
I'm convinced they are also killers
which is fine

We all have our vices

I wonder if they too wish to drown out all the light
and all the noise.

They never swim.

I swam today.

TO ANNE BOYLEN:

I wish I could sit with you
Your flesh would be severed
Around your neck
Your King's last mark upon you

You were once
As was I
The muse
The beauty
The lust

The catalyst
to a haughty man's betrayal

I read about you when I was 12
How your head was severed
from your body
The latter being touched far more often

I read about how your head rolled
into a basket
It would make me cry
and I would wipe away my tears
There was no black liner to smudge yet
There was no period to blame my emotions on

Yet I knew, in a raw way, what your body was

I would like to sit with you
and compare notes
as to when we watched the lust dim from their eyes
When good mornings turned into goodbyes
and when affection turned into abandonment

We both have our daughters

our prizes
Your Elizabeth
My Lila

I would tell you, Anne
To take comfort
Our girls will change the world

Yes
I'd like to sit with you
To show you
not too much has changed

KNUCKLES

I love my daughter's hands
More specifically, her knuckles.
Even more specifically,
the dimples that form above them.
Little wells.

I'll hold her hand
and trace my thumb over each one
Bringing to memory how I would play
with my grandma's aging veins
during church services.

I've scarred my own knuckles,
in one detrimental manner or another
I hope hers remain unscarred.

No fight
No pain
No purging out
No fear
No sadness

I'm sure my own mother
wanted the same for me.

I've fashioned my own hands
into more useful items now
Piggies to market
Counting numbers.

1, 2, 3,
3 again
until Lila learned 4
Shadow puppets

silly piano lessons.

My daughter has transformed her hands
into paws and runs around with the cats
purring and laughing at them.

I mentally take a snapshot.

One day, I will be old and wrinkly
I'm sure she will hold my hands
and notice the age.

We'll both think of our own
mortality and state how
the passage of time sped on too quickly

An obvious comment
one would make
much like the observation of weather

But now she is bordering on three
with all the adventures in front of her.
I'll interlace my fingers with hers
and we'll go together.

LJ

Dear Lila James,

I want you to know
the day I found out I was carrying you,
I felt whole again.
My heart stopped hurting,
and suddenly I wasn't so lonely anymore

That day, everything made more sense to me
I learned the reason I swept dark corners
of other's minds was so I could warn you
of the dangers when trying to save the devils out there

I can't promise you'll be happy every moment
I'm still trying to figure that out as well
But I promise to fight alongside you
While you find all the happiness you desire

I promise to look at you as a gift
that I never deserved
I promise to tell you stories each night
so your beautiful mind expands

I promise to encourage your curiosity
I promise to honor your individuality
I promise to protect you fiercely
from absolutely anyone who wishes you harm

This world isn't always beautiful
but I promise we'll find the beauty in it
and where there is darkness
we'll both shine all our light

Your mama is scared, little girl
I'm scared more times than not
but there's this thing called bravery
and we'll use that as our magic potion every morning

If your kind heart leads you to love monsters
I'll hold your hand while you do
knowing that music and hot cocoa won't fix
the heartache they may bring you

I want you to know that your worth isn't reflected
in your looks or your achievements
But in your spirit and your strength
In your words and your intentions

I want you to know something I wrote long ago
"you are not a lonely man's adventure or a sad man's escape."
You are enough, with all your complexities and quirks
I promise you are more precious than you'll believe

I promise to wake you up during every thunderstorm
with a bowl of ice cream
and we can watch the lightning dress up the sky
while I steal a bite of your Rocky Road

I promise to always laugh
when you place olives
on each one of your ten fingers
during Thanksgiving dinner
and I promise to demolish them all
if you don't have a taste for olives

I promise to always stand up for you
when you are belittled or demeaned
I promise that there will never be another soul on this earth
whose needs I'll put before yours

I will try to save you from so much sadness
that I have known before you entered this world
I promise not only to wipe away your tears
but to teach you how to get through the valley yourself

I promise you that there is nothing you could ever do
to make me love you any less
Your mama is full of mistakes
so I promise to introduce you to grace

I promise you Lila Bean
to do my best when it comes to you
I promise to admit fault, to apologize
to be grateful for each hiccup we go through

I'm a sloppy, spirited woman
You'll have your wildness too
but I promise you, unconditional love
L, you don't know how much I needed you.

SPLINTERS

I want her to feel like magic.
I want her to walk into a room with her head held high, eager to be seen.
I want her to think the moon shines only for her.
I want her to be so full of love that any pain she experiences
becomes a splinter rather than an amputation of her spirit.

Right now she tells me I'm a superhero.
I can see that if that superhero was Deadpool.

She tells me that she'll talk to a beaver
about biting her toenails down for her
so I don't have to clip them.

She tells me
"It's okay, try again"
when I make a simple mistake.

She tells people they're beautiful, unprompted.

Sometimes I can't believe she came from me.

No one really tells you how to raise an intact girl
when you, yourself were a broken girl for so many years.
It's complex and messy and easily the bravest quest I've been on.

I see the fire in her eyes and I find myself grieving already.
I know there will be moments when the fire dims
or will be extinguished
and it breaks my heart to know those times await her.

Today we drove into town
and went over the normal affirmations.
She is smart
Funny

Kind
Brave
Beautiful.

She tells me there was a friend
who called her "stupid."
I feel my rage catch in my throat
But this is about her, not me.
So I calmly say
"well that was a lie, wasn't it?
A mean lie.
Because you are smart,
you know so many things."

She agrees.

I let myself take my own advice.

In fact, I let myself believe
all the things I tell my daughter.
I'm magic.
I'm meant to be seen.
The moon shines for me.

And lately,
I feel so full of love,
that all that pain feels like a mere splinter...

HURRICANE GIRL

Dear Little Hurricane Girl,

You're a ledge-hopping, fire-breathing dragon in search of devouring each perfect princess you compare yourself to. You're a puzzle piece with cardboard frayed edges from being repeatedly shoved in the same incorrect placing.

Let me find you in your barefoot-swinging, Judy Garland drenched hideaway; tracing the outline of the tree's bark with your pointer finger, tempted to tear it away to see it, raw.

Exposed.

Let me sit beside you and distract your daydreams with some truths. Truths that will take you decades to learn.

Little girl, you were never meant to be perfect.

You need to know your own two hands are strong enough to hold your own heart. You'll find you can't search for answers at the end of bottles like you look for jokes on the end of popsicle sticks.
And boys' mouths aren't caves you explore...you won't find your adventures within them.
You need to know your body was not meant for abuse, not even your own. You cannot carve away your sadness like you copy Shel Silverstein's illustrations on a blank canvas.
It isn't art.
You're going to need to forgive yourself for all the terrible things you did to earn love.
You're going to fall asleep each night tucked in by a blanket of bitterness, and if you turn into it just right, it's going to feel just like your father's embrace.

You'll trade your pb&j's in for pain. And swap your dreams for disappointment.

Right now you twirl around in your living room until you grow dizzy and close your eyes to pretend you're Dorothy with the click-clack of her ruby heels. But you'll learn not to make friends with lions who look at you like their next meal. And if you were Alice, you wouldn't accidentally fall down a rabbit hole. You'd dive in head first just to see what would happen.
And the only magic mirror you'll end up wishing for is one that won't let you hate what's reflecting back at you.
And if you were little Red, you'd go back to the Wolf and invite him over for coffee every Thursday just to see if you could fix him.

But little hurricane girl, listen...
There will come a day when you'll learn to smile with the sunny sky, instead of screaming along with the stormy ones.
And you won't search for the "destruct" button on every chapter you find yourself in.
You'll learn that "letting it go" isn't a Banksy painted girl gently releasing a red balloon. But instead, it's taking a saw to the rusted chains that feel like fuzzy, mismatched socks around your ankles.
And you're still going to search for magic in the smallest of things.
Like when you can smell the rain on the pavement before the dewey drops appear visible.
Or in the creaking of antique doors, hinges worn, in buildings created centuries ago.
Or in the rustling of your favorite pages in the wind, as you're perched on a cliff.
Or in the 3:44 mark of your favorite Groban song, where you just want to plant yourself forever.
And while taking a seashell to your ear, because it sounds like the wind whistling through the hills before Maria sings on top of them.

You'll gently learn to love your own company. To still go after everything you want, and take yourself out of other people's stories.
You'll learn you are not a lonely man's adventure, or a sad man's escape.
You'll learn God never forsook you. He just knew His little girl was born a runner, even with her broken bones.

So go on and sit still with the homeless.
And talk out of turn.

And wonder what's around the corner...
or where that brush-covered path leads.
"Grow curious and curiouser."

And in the words of your sweet Cinderella,
"Have courage and be kind."

Because little hurricane girl,
out of all the wild, adventurous notions you'll have...
being happy will be your wildest.

ABOUT THE AUTHOR

Anna Schenck was born a free spirit into a life engulfed in restraint. Growing up in the PNW on an island in Washington state with her 2 siblings, Anna found herself surrounded by a small community and large religious influence. Words became an early escape from a life of confusion and chaos. She immersed herself in literature and film that allowed her to see a life beyond the little island she called home. By age 7, Anna was writing to make sense of her life experiences and navigate her way into the world. Anna has found her way back to that small island in Washington with a new sense of vigor. She is working as a nurse, continuing her education, still writing her way through life's challenges, and raising a fierce young woman to use her words too.

CPSIA information can be obtained
at www.ICGtesting.com
Printed in the USA
LVHW041525090723
751941LV00008B/973